LITTLE WOMEN

At Christmas the four March girls decide that they will all try hard to be good, and never to be cross, or lazy, or selfish again. Meg, the oldest, won't complain about her job or not having pretty dresses. Jo won't argue and get angry and run wild like a boy. Shy Beth will try hard to be braver, and little Amy will think less of herself and more of other people.

They don't always succeed, of course, and sometimes there are arguments and secrets and angry tears. But there is also laughter and fun, and soon a new friend – Laurie, the rich and lonely boy next door.

Many troubles and difficulties lie in the year ahead – and the girls are growing up. Wild Jo hates the idea of being a polite young lady, but Meg will soon be seventeen, and ready to fall in love . . .

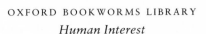

OXFORD BOOKWORMS LIBRARY
Human Interest

Little Women

Stage 4 (1400 headwords)

Series Editor: Jennifer Bassett
Founder Editor: Tricia Hedge
Activities Editors: Jennifer Bassett and Christine Lindop

LOUISA MAY ALCOTT

Little Women

Retold by
John Escott

Illustrated by
Martin Cottam

OXFORD UNIVERSITY PRESS

OXFORD
UNIVERSITY PRESS

Great Clarendon Street, Oxford OX2 6DP

Oxford University Press is a department of the University of Oxford.
It furthers the University's objective of excellence in research, scholarship,
and education by publishing worldwide in

Oxford New York

Auckland Cape Town Dar es Salaam Hong Kong Karachi
Kuala Lumpur Madrid Melbourne Mexico City Nairobi
New Delhi Shanghai Taipei Toronto

With offices in

Argentina Austria Brazil Chile Czech Republic France Greece
Guatemala Hungary Italy Japan South Korea Poland Portugal
Singapore Switzerland Thailand Turkey Ukraine Vietnam

OXFORD and OXFORD ENGLISH are registered trade marks of
Oxford University Press in the UK and in certain other countries

First published in Oxford Bookworms 1995
10 12 14 16 15 13 11 9

No unauthorized photocopying

Any websites referred to in this publication are in the public domain and
their addresses are provided by Oxford University Press for information only.
Oxford University Press disclaims any responsibility for the content

ISBN-13: 978 0 19 423036 0
ISBN-10: 0-19-423036-8

A complete recording of this Bookworms edition of
Little Women is available on cassette ISBN 0 19 422786 3

Typeset by Wyvern Typesetting Ltd, Bristol

Printed in Hong Kong

CONTENTS

1

Four sisters

'Christmas won't be Christmas without any presents,' said Jo crossly.

'It's so awful to be poor!' agreed Meg, looking at her old dress.

'It's not right for some girls to have pretty things, and others to have nothing at all,' said little Amy.

'We've got Father and Mother, and each other,' said Beth gently.

The four young faces round the fire cheered up as they thought of this, but then Jo said sadly, 'We haven't got Father, and we won't have him for a long time.' She didn't say 'perhaps never', but each silently thought it, remembering that he was away at the war in the South.

'Christmas won't be Christmas without any presents.'

Then Meg said, 'Mother says we shouldn't spend money on presents when our men are fighting a war.'

'We can't expect anything from Mother or each other,' said Jo, 'but we only have a dollar each, and that won't help the army much. Let's each buy ourselves what we want, and have a little fun. We work hard to earn it.'

'*I* do, teaching those awful children,' said Meg.

'What about me?' said Jo. 'I'm shut up all day working for a terrible old lady, who gives me different orders every five seconds!'

'I think washing cups and plates and keeping things tidy is the worst work in the world,' said Beth. 'My hands get too tired to play my music.'

'I have to go to school with girls who laugh at my dresses and say cruel things because my father isn't rich,' said Amy.

'I wish we had the money Father lost when we were little, Jo,' said Meg.

'I wish I was a boy,' said Jo. 'Then I could go and fight beside Father!'

Meg was sixteen and very pretty, with large eyes and soft brown hair, and white hands. Fifteen-year-old Jo was very tall and thin. Her long, dark-red hair was usually pushed up out of the way. Beth was thirteen, a very shy girl who seemed to live in a happy world of her own. Amy was the youngest, but thought herself to be the most important. She had blue eyes, and yellow hair which curled on to her shoulders.

At six o'clock, Beth put a pair of slippers by the fire to

warm and Meg lit the lamp. Amy got out of the comfortable chair without being asked, and Jo forgot how tired she was and held the slippers closer to the fire.

'These are old,' she said. 'Mother needs a new pair.'

Jo held the slippers closer to the fire.

'I'll get her some with my dollar,' said Beth.

'No, I shall!' cried Amy.

'I'm the oldest—' began Meg.

'I'm the man of the family now Father is away, and *I* shall buy them,' said Jo.

'Let's each get her something and not get anything for ourselves,' said Beth.

'That's a kind idea!' said Jo. 'What shall we get?'

Everyone thought for a moment, then Meg said, 'I'll give her a nice pair of gloves.'

'The best army slippers,' said Jo.

'Some handkerchiefs,' said Beth.

'A little bottle of perfume,' said Amy. 'It won't cost much, so I'll have some money left to buy something for me.'

'We'll let Mother think we're getting things for ourselves, and then surprise her,' said Jo.

Mrs March arrived home soon after. She took off her wet things and put on her warm slippers. Meg made the tea, Jo brought wood for the fire, Beth was quiet and busy, and Amy gave orders.

'I've got a letter from Father!' cried Mrs March.

It was a letter to cheer them up, and the special message for the girls came at the end: *Give them all my love and a kiss. I think of them every day. I know they will be loving children to you, and that when I come back, I will be prouder than ever of my little women.*

A tear dropped off the end of Jo's nose.

'A nice pair of gloves and some handkerchiefs.'

Amy hid her face on her mother's shoulder. 'I'm selfish,' she cried, 'but I'll try to be better.'

'We all will!' cried Meg. 'I think too much about the way I look, and hate to work, but I won't any more.'

'And I'll try to be a "little woman",' said Jo, 'and not be rough and wild.'

Beth said nothing, but she began to work hard at a blue army glove she was making.

So the four girls decided that they would all try very hard to be good. They would never be cross, or lazy, or selfish – and they would all help each other. They talked over their plan that evening, while they made sheets for Aunt March. Then at nine o'clock they stopped to sing a song. Beth played the old piano, and Meg and her mother led the singing. Jo always sang in the wrong place, but the girls never got too old to sing together.

2
A Happy Christmas

Jo was the first to wake up on Christmas morning, but soon they were all awake and they went downstairs.

'Where's Mother?' asked Meg.

'I don't know,' said old Hannah. She had lived with the family since Meg was born, and was more like a friend than a servant. 'Some poor woman came to the door and your mother went off to see what was needed.'

'She'll be back soon,' said Meg. She looked at the presents for her mother which were in a basket under a chair, ready to bring out at the right time. 'Where is Amy's bottle of perfume?'

'She went to put some pretty paper round it, I think,' said Jo.

Suddenly, they heard the outside door close.

'Here's Mother! Hide the basket, quick!' said Jo.

But it was Amy. She came in quickly.

'Where have you been, and what's that behind you?' asked Meg.

'I ran to the shop and changed the little bottle of perfume for a big one,' said Amy. 'I spent *all* my money to get it, and I'm not going to be selfish any more!'

Meg smiled proudly and put her arms around her sister. Then there was another bang from the outside door, and the basket was pushed back under the chair. The girls ran to the table, ready for their breakfast.

'Happy Christmas, Mother!' they shouted.

'Happy Christmas, little daughters!' said Mrs March.

Then the smile disappeared from her face. 'Girls, listen. Not far away is a poor woman, Mrs Hummel, with a new baby. Her six children are in one bed, trying to keep warm, as they have no wood for a fire. There is nothing to eat and they are hungry and cold. Will you give them your breakfast as a Christmas present?'

For a minute no one spoke. Then Jo said, 'Mother, I'm so glad you came back before we began to eat!' And the girls quickly began to put their breakfast in a basket.

'I knew you would do it,' said Mrs March, smiling.

She took the girls and Hannah to a cold, miserable little room in an old building, where they found a sick mother, a crying baby, and a group of children with white, frightened faces. The children were on the bed under a blanket, trying to keep warm.

The woman almost cried with happiness when she saw the girls. Hannah, who had brought wood, made a fire. Mrs March gave the mother tea and hot food, then she dressed the little baby gently. The girls put the children round the fire and fed them like hungry birds.

It was a very happy meal, although the girls ate none of it. But no one was happier than those hungry young ladies who gave away their breakfast on Christmas morning.

Mrs March was surprised and pleased when she saw her presents later. There was a lot of laughing and kissing and explaining. Then, for the rest of the day, the girls were busy. Jo liked to write plays, and the four of them were going to act one that evening. They had learned their words, and had worked hard to make strange and wonderful clothes for all the different characters in the play.

On Christmas night, some other girls came to watch. At first, there was a lot of whispering and laughing from the four sisters behind the curtains. Then the curtains were opened and the play began.

It was an exciting story about Hugo (acted by Jo wearing a black beard!), beautiful Zara and brave Roderigo. There were also two ghosts, a cruel king, and a tall castle made of paper and wood – which unfortunately fell down just as Roderigo and Zara were escaping from it. There were screams of laughter from everyone, but the actors picked themselves up and carried on through more dangers and mysteries until the happy ending was reached.

All the visitors loved the play, and after the excitement and fun came a surprise for everyone.

'Would the young ladies like to stay for supper?' asked Hannah.

And when the girls saw the supper table, they could not believe their eyes! There was ice-cream, cake, fruit, and French chocolate! And in the middle of the table were flowers for each of the four actors.

'Where did it all come from?' asked Amy.

'From Father Christmas, perhaps?' said Beth.

'Mother did it,' said Meg.

The castle fell down as Roderigo and Zara were escaping from it.

'Aunt March sent it,' said Jo.

'You're all wrong,' laughed Mrs March. 'Old Mr Laurence sent it!'

'The Laurence boy's grandfather?' said Meg. 'But we don't know him.'

'Hannah told his servant about your breakfast party, and that pleased him,' said Mrs March. 'He knew my father many years ago, and he sent me a note this afternoon, asking if he could send my children a few small Christmas presents.'

'The idea came from that boy, I know it did!' said Jo. 'I'm sure he wants to know us, but he's shy, and Meg won't let me speak to him when we pass him in the street. She says that it's not at all polite for young ladies to introduce themselves to strangers.'

'You mean the people who live in the big house next door, don't you?' said one of the other girls. 'My mother knows old Mr Laurence. She says he keeps his grandson in the house when the boy isn't riding or walking with his tutor, and makes him study very hard. We invited the boy to our party but he didn't come.'

'That boy needs to have some fun,' said Jo.

3

The Laurence boy

'Look!' said Meg, excitedly, a day or two later. She waved a piece of paper at Jo. 'An invitation to a New Year's party at Sallie Gardiner's house, and it's for both of us. Mother says we can go, but what shall we wear?'

'Our best cotton dresses,' said Jo, 'because we haven't got anything else. Yours is as good as new, but mine has a burn and a hole in the back.'

'Then you must keep your back out of sight,' said Meg. 'I'll have a new ribbon for my hair, and my new slippers. And my gloves are all right.'

'Mine are stained, so I'll have to go without.'

'You *must* wear gloves to a dance, Jo!' cried Meg.

'Then we'll each wear one good one and carry a bad one,' said Jo.

Meg looked worried. 'All right, but you will behave nicely, won't you? Don't stare, or put your hands behind your back.'

On New Year's Eve, the two younger sisters watched the two older girls get ready for the party. There was a lot of running up and down, and laughing and talking. Meg wanted some curls around her face, so Jo began to work on the papered ends of Meg's hair with a pair of hot tongs.

'Should they smoke like that?' asked Beth.

'It's the wetness drying,' said Jo.

'What a strange burning smell!' said Amy.

'I'll take the papers off now,' said Jo, 'and you'll see lots of little curls.'

She took the papers off – and, to her horror, the burnt hair came off with them!

'Oh, oh! What *have* you done to my hair!' cried Meg.

'I always get things wrong,' said Jo unhappily. 'I'm so sorry. I suppose the tongs were too hot.'

'I always get things wrong,' said Jo unhappily.

'Don't worry,' Amy told Meg, who was crying. 'Just tie your ribbon so that the ends come on to your forehead a little, and it will look quite fashionable.'

At last, Meg and Jo were ready and went off to the Gardiners' house where Mrs Gardiner welcomed them kindly. Meg immediately began to enjoy herself with Sallie, but Jo wasn't interested in girlish talk and stood with her back carefully against the wall, watching the dancing. Soon Meg was asked to dance, then Jo saw a big red-haired boy coming towards her and she quickly went through a door into a small room. Unfortunately, another shy person was already hiding there and she found herself looking at the 'Laurence boy'.

'Oh dear, I didn't know anyone was here!' Jo said.

The boy laughed. 'Don't go. I came in here because I don't know any people, but I think I've seen you before,' he said. 'You live near us, don't you?'

'Next door,' said Jo. 'We enjoyed your nice Christmas present.'

'My grandfather sent it, Miss March.'

'But you gave your grandfather the idea, didn't you, Mr Laurence?'

'I'm not Mr Laurence, only Laurie,' he said.

'And I'm not Miss March, only Jo,' she said. 'Do you like parties?'

'Sometimes,' he answered. 'I've been abroad a lot recently, and I don't know how you do things here.'

'Abroad!' said Jo. 'Oh, did you go to Paris?'

'We went there last winter.'

'Can you speak French?' she asked.

He said something in French, and Jo listened carefully. 'You asked, "Who is the young lady in the pretty slippers?" It's my sister, Meg, and you knew it was! Do you think she's pretty?'

'Yes,' he said. 'She looks so fresh and quiet.'

This pleased Jo very much, and soon the two of them were talking easily, like old friends. 'I hear you're always studying hard,' said Jo. 'Are you going to college soon?'

'Not for a year or two,' he said. 'I'm sixteen next month, and I won't go before I'm seventeen.'

'I wish I was going to college,' said Jo.

'I hate even the idea of it!' said Laurie.

Jo wanted to know why, but he looked so serious that instead of asking she said, 'Why don't you go and dance?'

'I will if you'll come too,' he answered.

'I can't because—' Jo stopped.

'Because what?'

'You won't tell?'

'Never!'

'I've a bad habit of standing near a fire, and I burn my dresses,' said Jo. 'I have to keep still so that no one will see the burn on this one. Laugh if you like.'

But Laurie didn't laugh. 'Never mind that,' he said gently. 'Please come.'

Jo smiled. 'All right,' she said. 'Thank you.'

When the music stopped, they sat down and began to talk, but Jo saw Meg waving at her. She went over and followed her sister into a side room.

'I've turned my foot over and hurt my ankle,' said Meg. 'I can't walk on it, and I don't know how I'm going to get home.'

'I'm not surprised you turned your foot over in those

stupid high shoes,' said Jo. 'You'll have to get a carriage or stay here all night.'

'A carriage will cost a lot,' said Meg, 'and I can't stay here for the night because the house is full. I'll just rest until Hannah comes to fetch us, then do the best I can.'

'They're going in for supper now,' said Jo. 'I'll stay with you.'

'No, run and bring me some coffee,' said Meg.

Jo found the coffee, but immediately dropped some down the front of her dress. She was cleaning it off with Meg's glove when a friendly voice spoke to her.

'Can I help?' said Laurie. He had a cup of coffee in one hand and a plate with a cake on it in the other.

'I was trying to get something for Meg,' said Jo.

'And I was looking for someone to give this to,' he said. He fetched more coffee and a cake for Jo, then the three of them had a happy time talking together until Hannah arrived. Meg completely forgot about her foot and stood up quickly. She cried out with pain, and when Laurie saw that she could not walk, he immediately offered to take them home in his grandfather's carriage.

'But you can't want to go home yet,' said Jo.

'I always go early,' said Laurie.

He sat with the driver, and the two girls sat with Hannah inside the carriage and talked excitedly about the party.

'I had a wonderful time, did you?' said Jo.

'Yes, until I hurt myself,' said Meg. 'Sallie's friend, Annie Moffat, has asked me to go and stay with her for a week in

the spring, when Sallie does.'

Jo told Meg her adventures, and then they were home. They thanked Laurie and went quietly into the house, hoping to wake no one. But as soon as they opened their bedroom door, two little voices cried out: 'Tell us about the party! Tell us about the party!'

⚮4⚮
The house next door

'It's so nice to go to parties and drive home in carriages,' said Meg, the next morning. 'Other people live like that all the time, and I wish we could. I wish we were rich.'

'Well, we're not,' said Jo. 'So we must do our work with a smile, the way Mother does.'

Mr March had lost most of his money helping a friend. When the two older girls discovered this, they wanted to

Laurie took them home in his grandfather's carriage.

do something to earn some money for the family, and as soon as they were old enough, they found work. Meg got a job teaching four small children. It was hard for her to be poor because she could remember the time when their home had been beautiful, with everything they wanted. And every day at Mrs King's house she saw pretty dresses, and heard talk of parties and the theatre – all the things which Meg loved.

Jo went to Aunt March, who needed someone to fetch and carry things, and read to her. She was a difficult old lady who complained a lot, but Jo did her best.

Beth was much too shy to go to school with other children, so she studied at home with her father. When he went away, and her mother was busy with war work, Beth continued to study by herself and helped Hannah keep the home tidy for the others. She also spent long, quiet hours alone, talking to her dolls or playing the old piano. Beth loved music and, although the family could not afford music lessons or a good piano for her, she tried hard to make herself a better musician.

Amy drew the most beautiful pictures and wanted to be a famous painter one day. She was a favourite with everyone, except when she complained about having to wear her cousin's old clothes because her mother could not afford to buy new ones for her.

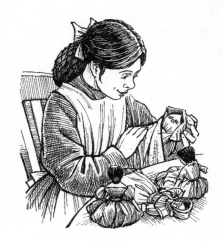

Beth spent hours alone, playing with her dolls.

One afternoon a week or two later, Jo went outside to clear the snow away from some of the garden so that Beth could walk there when the sun came out. She looked across to the house next door – a big stone house with lovely things inside that Jo occasionally saw through the open curtains at the windows. But it seemed a lonely, lifeless kind of house, as no children played outside, no motherly face smiled at the windows, and not many people went in and out, except the old gentleman and his grandson.

She had not seen the Laurence boy lately and wondered if he was away, but suddenly she saw him looking out of an upstairs window. She threw up a handful of soft snow and called out, 'Are you ill?'

Laurie opened the window. 'I'm almost better, thank you,' he said. 'I've had a bad cold.'

'What do you find to do?' said Jo.

'Nothing,' he said. 'They won't let me.'

'Why don't you get someone to come and see you?'

'I don't know anyone.'

'You know us,' said Jo.

'So I do!' laughed Laurie. 'Will you come, please?'

'I'll come if Mother will let me. I'll go and ask her. Shut the window and wait until I come.'

Laurie was excited and began to get ready for Jo's visit. He brushed his hair and tried to make his room tidy. Soon after, he heard voices downstairs, then a surprised servant ran up to his room.

'There's a young lady to see you, sir,' she said.

A moment later, Jo appeared with a box in one hand and Beth's three small cats in the other. 'Mother sends her love,' she said. 'Meg asked me to bring some of her cake, and Beth thought you would like to play with her cats. Isn't she funny?'

Laurie laughed. 'How kind you all are,' he said.

'Shall I read to you?' said Jo.

'I'd rather talk,' he said.

'I can talk all day,' said Jo, smiling. 'Beth says I never know when to stop.'

'Is Beth the one who stays at home?'

'Yes, that's Beth. She's a good girl.'

'The pretty one is Meg, and the curly-haired one is Amy, is that right?' he said.

'Yes. How did you know?'

Laurie's face became red. 'I hear you calling to each other, and you always seem to be having so much fun. Sometimes, in the evenings, you forget to close your curtains and I can see you sitting round the fire with your mother. I haven't got a mother.'

Jo saw the sadness in his eyes. 'Why don't you come over and see us? Would your grandfather let you?'

'Perhaps, if your mother asked him,' said Laurie. 'He spends a lot of time among his books, and Mr Brooke, my tutor, doesn't live here. So I haven't anyone to go out with. Do you like your school?'

'I don't go to school. I go out to work – to my aunt's,' said Jo. She described the difficult old lady and made him laugh with her stories. She told him all about her sisters, the plays they acted, and their hopes and fears for their father. Then they talked about books, and Jo discovered that Laurie loved them as much as she did.

'Come and see our library,' he said. 'Grandfather is out, so you needn't be afraid.'

'I'm not afraid of anything,' replied Jo.

He took her down to a room where the walls were covered with books and pictures.

'You should be the happiest boy in the world!' said Jo, sitting in a big armchair and looking round.

'A person can't live on books,' he said.

Suddenly, a bell rang.

Jo jumped up out of the chair. 'It's your grandfather!' she said.

'What if it is?' said Laurie, with a smile. 'You're not afraid of anything, remember?'

'Perhaps I am a *little* bit afraid of him,' said Jo.

The servant came in at that moment. 'The doctor is here to see you, sir,' she said to Laurie.

'Can I leave you for a minute or two, Jo?' he said.

'Yes, I'm very happy here,' said Jo.

He went away and Jo was staring at a large picture of the old gentleman when the door opened again. Without turning, she said, 'I won't be afraid of him, because he's got kind eyes, although his mouth looks hard and cold. He's not as handsome as my grandfather, but I like him.'

'Thank you,' said a deep voice behind her.

She turned quickly – and saw old Mr Laurence!

Jo's face turned a bright red and she wanted to run away. But the old man's eyes looked kinder than those in the picture and seemed to have a smile in them.

'So you're not afraid of me, eh?' he said.

'Not much, sir.'

'But I'm not as handsome as your grandfather?'

'Not quite, sir.'

'But you like me.' He laughed and shook hands with her. 'Now, what have you been doing with my grandson?'

'Trying to cheer him up, sir,' said Jo. 'He seems a bit lonely.'

'Then come and have some tea with us.'

Laurie was very surprised to see Jo with his grandfather, but was soon talking and laughing happily with Jo. The old man watched the two young people and noticed the change in his grandson. 'She's right,' he thought. 'The boy *does* need cheering up.'

After tea, they went into a room where there was a large and beautiful piano.

'Do you play?' Jo asked Laurie.

'Sometimes,' he answered.

'Play now. I want to hear it so I can tell Beth.'

So Laurie played and Jo listened. Afterwards, Mr Laurence said, 'He plays quite well, but I want him to do well in more important things. Now, I hope you'll come again.' He shook hands with her. 'Goodnight, Jo.'

Laurie walked to the door with her. 'He doesn't like to hear me play,' he said.

'Why not?' said Jo.

'I'll tell you one day,' he said.

When Jo told the family of her afternoon's adventures, they all wanted to go and visit the big house.

'Mother, why doesn't Mr Laurence like to hear Laurie play the piano?' asked Jo.

'Laurie's father married an Italian lady, a musician,' said Mrs March. 'The old man didn't like her, and never saw his son after they were married. Laurie was born in Italy, but his parents died when he was a child, and his

Laurie played and Jo listened.

grandfather brought him home. Laurie loves music and I expect his grandfather is afraid he'll want to be a musician like his mother.'

'Laurie should be a musician if he wants to be,' said Jo. 'Sending him to college will just make him unhappy.'

5
A surprise for Beth

Laurie and the four girls were soon great friends. Mr Brooke complained to the old gentleman that his student was always running across to see the Marches.

'Let him have a bit of a holiday,' said Mr Laurence. 'He can catch up with his studies later.'

What good times they had! Writing and acting plays, happy evenings at the Marches, and little parties at the big house. Only Beth was too shy to go there. When Mr Laurence heard about Beth's shyness, he came to have tea with their mother one day, and began to talk about music and great singers he had heard. Beth found it impossible to stay in her corner and came to listen.

'Laurie hasn't much time for his music,' Mr Laurence told Mrs March, 'so the piano is not used very often. Would any of your girls like to play it sometimes? They needn't see or speak to anyone, and I'll be in my study.' He got up to go. 'But if they don't want to come . . .'

At this moment, a little hand touched his own. It was

Beth's. 'I – I want to come,' she said, her voice shaking. 'Very much.'

'You're the musical girl,' said Mr Laurence, gently.

'I'm Beth. Yes, I love music, and I shall come.'

The next day, Beth waited until the old and the young gentlemen both went out, then she ran across to the big house and found her way to the room with the beautiful piano. As soon as she began to play, she forgot her fears immediately in the delight which the music gave her.

After that, Beth went every day. She never knew that Mr Laurence often opened his study door to hear her playing, or that Laurie stood in the hall to keep the servants away from the shy little girl. But she was so grateful that she asked her mother and sisters to help her make the old gentleman a pair of slippers. After several days' careful sewing, the slippers were finished. Then Beth wrote a short letter and, with Laurie's help, left it with the slippers in the old man's study one morning, before he was up.

The next day, Beth went out for a walk, and when she came back the others were waiting for her. 'Here's a letter for you, Beth!' they called out. 'Come and read it!' She hurried to the house and they took her into the front room. 'Look there!' everyone was saying at once. Beth looked – and got the biggest surprise of her life! For there stood a lovely little piano, with a letter on the top of it, addressed to: 'Miss Elizabeth March'.

'You – you read it, Jo,' whispered Beth. 'I can't.'

So Jo opened the letter and began to read.

'*Dear Miss March,*' she read, '*I have had many pairs of slippers but none which have pleased me so much as yours. I should like to thank you for your kindness by sending you something that once belonged to my little granddaughter, who died. With many thanks. I am your good friend, James Laurence.*'

Jo put an arm around her sister. 'Now try it, Beth,' she said.

Beth sat down and began to play, and everyone thought it was the most perfect piano they had ever heard.

'You'll have to go and thank him,' said Jo, with a smile, knowing that Beth was much too shy to do anything like that.

But Beth surprised them all. 'I'll do it at once,' she said bravely, and away she walked, through the garden and into the big house next door. She went up to the old gentleman's study and knocked on the door.

'Come in,' said Mr Laurence.

Beth went in. 'I came to say thank you, sir,' she began, in her quiet little voice. But he looked so friendly that she ran and put both her arms around his neck and kissed him.

The old gentleman was so surprised that he nearly fell off his chair. But he was very pleased indeed by that shy little kiss, and soon the two of them were talking like old friends. Later, he walked home with Beth. The girls, watching with great interest from the window, could not believe their eyes. 'Well,' Meg said, 'I do believe the world is coming to an end!'

6

Amy in trouble

'Where are you going?' Amy asked Meg and Jo one afternoon. 'I want to come, too.'

'You can't, dear, you're not invited,' said Meg.

'You're going somewhere with Laurie, I know you are!'

'Yes, we are,' said Jo. 'Now stop annoying us.'

'You're going to the theatre!' Amy said suddenly. 'I want to go with you!'

'We could take her, I suppose,' began Meg.

'No, Laurie only invited us,' said Jo.

'I *shall* go,' shouted Amy. 'Meg says I can.'

'You just stay where you are!' said Jo, angrily.

'I'll make you sorry for this, Jo March!' Amy shouted, as Meg and Jo left the house.

The two older sisters enjoyed themselves at the theatre, but Jo couldn't stop worrying as she wondered what Amy would do to 'make her sorry'.

She found out the next afternoon.

Beth, Amy and Meg were sitting together when Jo ran into the room. 'Has anyone taken my notebook?' Jo asked.

Meg and Beth said 'No' at once, but Amy said nothing.

'Amy, you've got it,' said Jo.

'No, I haven't,' said Amy.

'That's a lie!' said Jo. 'Tell me the truth, or I'll make you!'

27

'Do what you like,' said Amy. 'You'll never see your stupid book again, because I burned it!'

Jo's face went white. 'What! But I worked so hard writing my stories!'

'I said I'd make you sorry, and I have!' said Amy.

Jo jumped at Amy and shook her shoulders. 'You wicked, wicked girl!' cried Jo. 'I'll never, ever forgive you!' And she ran out of the room.

Mrs March came home and heard the story.

'Oh, how could you do that, Amy?' she said. 'That was Jo's book of stories. She wrote them all herself, and was hoping to make them good enough to print.'

Slowly, Amy began to understand the terrible thing she had done, and started to cry. Later, when Jo appeared for tea, Amy begged her sister to forgive her.

'I shall never forgive you,' Jo answered.

It was not a happy evening, and when singing time came, Jo remained silent. Afterwards, she kissed her mother and said 'Goodnight'.

'My dear, don't go to bed feeling so angry with your sister,' whispered Mrs March.

'I'm sorry, Mother, I can't forgive her,' replied Jo.

Next day, Jo wanted to get out of the house, so she picked up her skates and went next door to ask Laurie to take her skating.

Amy heard them going. 'Jo promised to take me with her next time!' she complained.

'It's hard for her to forgive you, Amy,' said Meg. 'Go

after them and wait until Jo is enjoying herself, then give her a kiss or do something kind.'

It was not far to the river, but Jo and Laurie were already skating when Amy arrived. Jo saw Amy but turned away. Laurie was carefully skating along the edge of the ice and didn't see the younger girl.

Amy put her skates on and stood on the ice.

'Keep near the edge. The ice isn't safe in the middle,' Laurie called to Jo, then he disappeared round the first bend in the river.

Jo heard, but Amy did not. Jo realized that Amy probably hadn't heard, but she said nothing and skated after Laurie. 'Let Amy look after herself!' Jo thought.

Amy skated out towards the smoother ice in the middle of the river. Jo reached the bend, and for a moment she stood still, a strange feeling in her heart. Something made her turn round – just in time to see Amy throw up her hands and go crashing through the ice into the cold water! Amy gave a cry that make Jo's heart stop with fear. She tried to call Laurie, but her voice was gone, and for a second she could only stand and stare at the little blue hood of Amy's coat above the black water.

Suddenly, Laurie skated past her and shouted, 'Bring a piece of wood from the side of the river, quickly!'

Wild with fear, Jo fetched some wood and pulled it across the ice, while Laurie held Amy's head above the water. Together, they got her out.

She was more frightened than hurt, and was quickly

Jo saw Amy crash through the ice into the cold water.

taken home. They covered her in blankets and tried to calm her, and after a little while she fell asleep in front of the warm fire. Later, when everything was quiet, Jo asked her mother, 'Are you sure she's safe?'

'Quite safe, dear. It was sensible to get her home as quickly as you did.'

'Laurie did it all,' said Jo. 'Mother, if she should die, it will be my fault. I get angry so quickly. Oh, why can't I be more like you?'

'I get angry nearly every day of my life, Jo,' said Mrs

March, 'but I've learned not to show it. I've learned to stop myself saying the angry words that come to my lips, and you must try to do the same, my dear.'

Amy moved in her sleep and Jo looked at her. 'I refused to forgive her, and today, she nearly died! And it was Laurie who saved her. How could I be so wicked?' Jo began to cry.

Then Amy opened her eyes and held out her arms, with a smile that went straight to Jo's heart. Neither of them said a word, but they held each other close, and everything was forgiven and forgotten.

7

Meg hears some gossip

Annie Moffat did not forget her promised invitation, and one April day Meg went to stay at the Moffats' large house. Meg thought it was wonderful. She loved riding in fine carriages, wearing her best dress every day, and doing nothing except enjoy herself. She soon began to talk about fashionable clothes and hairstyles in the way that the other girls did. And the more Meg saw of Annie's pretty things, the more she wished that she, too, was rich.

Annie's older sisters, Belle and Clara, were fine young ladies; Mr Moffat was a fat, friendly gentleman; and Mrs Moffat was a fat, friendly lady. They were all very kind to Meg and did their best to make her feel at home.

When the evening for a 'small party' came, Meg's best dress looked very old next to Sallie's new one, but no one said anything about it. The girls were getting ready when a servant brought in a box of flowers.

'For Miss March,' she said. 'And here's a letter.'

'What fun! Who are they from?' said the girls. 'We didn't know you had a young man.'

'The letter is from Mother and the flowers are from Laurie,' said Meg, simply.

'Oh,' said Annie, with a strange look.

Her mother's loving words and Laurie's kindness made Meg feel much happier and she enjoyed the party very much. Annie made her sing, and someone said that Meg had a fine voice. So Meg was having a nice time – until she heard someone say, on the other side of a large table of flowers: 'How old is the Laurence boy?'

'Sixteen or seventeen, I think,' said another voice.

'It would be an excellent thing for one of those girls,' said a third voice. 'Sallie says they are very friendly, and the old man thinks they are all wonderful.'

'I expect Mrs M. has made her plans,' said Mrs Moffat's voice, 'but do you think the girl knows of them?'

'She told that little lie about her mother, and her cheeks went pink. I'm sure the note was from the boy really. Poor thing! She'd be very pretty if she had some nice clothes. Do you think she'll mind if we offer to lend her a dress for Thursday?'

'I shall ask young Laurence to come, and we'll have some fun with her afterwards.'

Meg tried to forget what she'd heard, but could not. The gossip made her angry, and she was glad when the party was over and she was alone in her bed. She cried quietly to herself. Why did people have to say those things? She and Laurie were just friends, but now that friendship felt damaged by the unkind gossip.

The next day, Miss Belle said, 'Meg, dear, we've sent an invitation to your friend, Mr Laurence, for Thursday.'

Meg pretended to misunderstand. 'You're very kind, but I'm afraid he won't come. He's nearly seventy.'

Miss Belle laughed. 'I mean the *young* man.'

'There isn't one,' said Meg. 'Laurie is only a boy.'

'Isn't he about your age?' said Clara.

'Nearer Jo's,' said Meg. 'I'm seventeen in August.'

'It's nice of him to send you flowers,' said Annie.

'He often does, to all of us,' said Meg. 'My mother and old Mr Laurence are friends, you know.'

'What will you wear on Thursday?' asked Sallie.

'My white dress again, I haven't got any others.'

'No others?' said Sallie. 'How funny—'

'I have a pretty blue dress I can't wear any more, Meg,' said Belle. 'It will please me if you wear it.'

'You're very kind, but—,' began Meg.

'Please, do,' said Belle. 'You'll look quite beautiful in it.'

Meg couldn't refuse this kind offer and, on the Thursday evening, Belle helped to change Meg into a fine lady. She brushed and curled her hair, reddened her lips, then helped her to get into the sky-blue dress. The neck of the dress was cut very low, and Meg was quite shocked when she saw herself in the mirror. A necklace and earrings were added, and Meg was ready for the party.

At first, she felt strange in all the fine clothes, but she soon discovered that people who did not usually notice her now came to speak to her. Several young men who had only stared before now asked to be introduced.

Suddenly, Meg saw Laurie across the room. He was staring at her, and he didn't look very pleased. Meg began to feel uncomfortable, and she wished that she had worn her old dress. As she walked up to Laurie, she saw Belle

Meg was ready for the party.

and Annie watching them both and smiling.

'I'm glad you came,' Meg said to Laurie, in her most grown-up voice. 'I was afraid you wouldn't.'

'Jo wanted me to come and tell her how you looked,' said Laurie.

'What will you tell her?'

'I'll say I didn't know you, because you look so unlike yourself. I'm quite afraid of you,' he said.

'The girls dressed me up for fun,' said Meg. 'Don't you like it?'

'No, I don't,' came the cool reply.

Meg became angry. 'Then I shan't stay with you!' And she walked off towards the window.

A moment or two later, an older man went past her and she heard him say to his friend, 'That girl has been dressed up like a doll.'

'Oh dear,' thought Meg. 'Why didn't I wear my own things?'

She turned and saw Laurie behind her. 'Please forgive me,' he said. 'Come and have something to eat.'

Meg tried to look annoyed.

'Please come,' he said again. 'I don't like your dress, but I do think you are – wonderful.'

Meg smiled and found it impossible to stay angry with him. 'Please don't tell them at home about my dress,' she said. 'They won't understand that it was just for fun, and it will worry Mother. I was stupid to wear it, but I'll tell them myself.'

'I won't say anything,' he promised.

He did not see her again until supper time, when she was drinking wine with two other boys.

'You'll feel ill tomorrow, if you drink much of that, Meg,' Laurie whispered to her.

'I'm not Meg tonight,' she said. 'I'm a doll who does crazy things. Tomorrow, I'll be good again.'

Meg danced and laughed and talked to as many young men as she could manage, but went to bed feeling that she hadn't enjoyed herself as much as she had expected.

She was sick all the next day, and on Saturday went home, quite tired of her fortnight's fun.

'I'm glad to be home,' she said to her mother and Jo, after telling them how she was dressed up like a doll, drank too much wine, and was ill afterwards. She had laughed while telling them the story, but her face still looked worried at the end.

'There is something else, I think,' said Mrs March, smoothing Meg's cheek, which suddenly became rose-red.

'Yes,' Meg said slowly. 'I hate people saying and thinking awful things about us and Laurie.' Then she told them the gossip she had heard.

'What rubbish!' said Jo. 'Just wait until *I* see Annie Moffat! How stupid to think that Mother has "plans", and that we are kind to Laurie because he is rich and may marry one of us one day. He'll laugh when I tell him!'

'No, Jo,' said her mother. 'You must never repeat wicked gossip.'

'*Do* you have "plans", Mother?' asked Meg.

'All mothers do, dear,' said Mrs March. 'But my plans are different from Mrs Moffat's, I suspect. I want my daughters to be loved, and I want people to think well of them. I want them to marry well, but not to marry rich men just because they are rich. I'd rather you were poor men's wives, if that meant you had happy, peaceful lives. But your father and I believe that we'll always be proud of our daughters, whether they are married or single.'

'You will, you will!' said Meg and Jo, together.

8

All play and no work

'The first of June, and the King family is going on holiday tomorrow!' said Meg. 'I'm free for three months!'

'And Aunt March went away for her holiday today,' said Jo. 'Isn't life wonderful!'

'What will you do all your holiday?' asked Amy.

'I'll stay in bed late, and do nothing,' said Meg.

'I have lots of books to read,' said Jo.

'Let's not do any studying, Beth,' said Amy. 'Let's play all the time, and rest, as Jo and Meg are going to do.'

'I will if Mother doesn't mind,' said Beth.

Mrs March agreed to the plan and said they could try it for a week.

'But,' she added, 'I think by Saturday night you will find

that all play and no work is as bad as all work and no play.'

Next day, Meg appeared at ten o'clock and ate breakfast alone. It was a lonely meal and the room was untidy, because Beth had not cleaned it.

Jo went to the river with Laurie, then sat in the apple tree and read a book. Beth began to tidy things in her cupboard, but she got tired and left it half-done. She went to her piano, glad that she did not have to wash the cups and plates. Amy sat in the garden to draw, hoping someone would see her and say something nice about her picture. But no one appeared, so she went for a walk, got caught in the rain and came home very wet.

At tea, everyone said that it had been a delightful but unusually long day. Meg, who had been shopping in the afternoon, now decided that she did not like the dress she had bought. Jo had a headache from reading too long. Beth couldn't find anything in her cupboard, and the rain had made Amy's dress so wet that she couldn't wear it to Katy Brown's party the next day.

Mrs March listened, smiled and said nothing.

The week seemed to get longer and longer with nothing much to do, and by Friday the girls were glad that it was nearly over. Then Mrs March gave Hannah a holiday, and when the girls got up on Saturday, there was no breakfast ready, no fire in the kitchen, and no mother waiting for them.

'What has happened?' said Jo.

Meg ran upstairs, then came down to say that Mother

was staying in her room to have a rest. 'She says we must look after ourselves today,' Meg said.

'Good, I want something to do,' said Jo.

Secretly, they were all pleased to have something useful to do again. Beth and Amy put cups and plates on the table while Jo and Meg got the breakfast, then Meg took some tea and an egg up to Mrs March. The tea was too strong and the egg was burned. Mrs March did not complain, but she laughed to herself afterwards.

Jo decided to invite Laurie to dinner. 'There's meat and vegetables and plenty of potatoes,' she told Meg, 'and we can have strawberries, and then coffee.' Her mother said she did not mind at all because she was going out for dinner.

Jo did her best, but the potatoes were still hard in the middle, the vegetables were cooked too long and fell to pieces, and the meat was burned black. The strawberries were not ready for eating, and she put salt on them instead of sugar! Unfortunately, this was not discovered until Laurie began eating them. He pretended everything was all right, but Amy took a spoonful and ran from the table.

'What's wrong?' said Jo.

Meg and Laurie told her. 'Oh, no!' said Jo. Then she saw Laurie start to smile, and she began to laugh. Soon everyone was laughing with her.

'What a terrible day!' said Jo, after they had cleared everything away.

Mrs March returned home later. 'Have you enjoyed your

Amy ran from the table.

week of all play and no work, girls, or do you want another week of it?' she said.

'I don't!' said Jo.

'Nor do I!' shouted the others.

'Mother, did you go out and leave us just to see how we would manage?' asked Meg.

'Yes,' said Mrs March. 'I wanted you to see that being comfortable depends on us all helping each other and not just thinking of ourselves. Isn't it better to have time for play *and* time for work, and to make each day useful and enjoyable?'

'Oh, it is, Mother, it is!' said the girls.

Some days later, all four girls went on a picnic with Laurie and his tutor, Mr Brooke, and some other young people. Sallie Gardiner and her English friend, Miss Kate Vaughn, were among them. It was a sunny day and they had their picnic on a hill, under some trees.

After the meal, most of the young ladies and gentlemen played games, but Miss Kate sat under a tree and began to draw. Meg watched, while Mr Brooke lay on the grass beside her, with a book which he did not read.

'I wish I could draw,' said Meg.

'Why don't you learn?' replied Miss Kate. She was a little older than the other girls and was very much the fashionable young lady.

'I haven't time,' said Meg. 'I have a job, teaching four children in a family.'

'Oh!' said Miss Kate, looking rather shocked. She said no more, but her face showed that she thought being a private teacher was little better than being a servant, and Meg's cheeks quickly became red.

'In America, young ladies prefer to work and earn money for themselves,' said Mr Brooke quickly, 'and not expect others to pay for everything.'

'I see,' said Miss Kate, coldly. Soon after, she took her drawing and moved away.

'There's no place like America for us workers, Miss Meg,' said Mr Brooke, smiling. His brown eyes looked at Meg warmly, and she smiled back at him.

'I wish I liked teaching as much as you do,' she said.

'You would if you were teaching Laurie,' said Mr Brooke. 'I'll be sorry when he goes to college next year. But then I shall become a soldier.'

'I think every young man wants to be a soldier,' said Meg, 'but it's hard for the family who stay at home.'

'I have no family, and not many friends to care if I live or die,' said Mr Brooke, sadly.

'Laurie and his grandfather would care,' said Meg, 'and we would all be very sorry if anything happened to you.'

'Thank you,' said Mr Brooke, cheering up immediately.

Secrets

One October afternoon, Jo caught a bus into the town and stopped outside a building in one of the busy streets. She went in, looked up the stairs and, after a minute, ran out again. She did this several times, to the great amusement of a young man who was watching from the opposite side of the road. But the fourth time, Jo gave herself a shake and walked up the stairs.

The young man crossed the road and waited. It was Laurie. Ten minutes later, Jo came running out, but did not look pleased to see him.

'What are you doing here?' she said.

'I'm waiting to walk home with you,' he said. 'I've a secret to tell you, but first you must tell me yours.'

'You won't say anything at home, will you?' said Jo.

'Not a word,' promised Laurie.

'I've left two of my stories with a newspaper man,' said Jo, 'but I'll have to wait until next week before I know if they will be printed.'

'Miss March, the famous American writer!' said Laurie, throwing his hat into the air and catching it.

Jo looked pleased. 'Now, what's *your* secret?'

'You remember Meg lost a glove at the picnic?' said Laurie. 'Well, I know where it is.'

'Is that all?' said Jo, looking disappointed.

'Wait until I tell you *where* it is,' he said.

'Tell me then,' said Jo.

Laurie whispered three words in Jo's ear.

She stared at him, looking both surprised and displeased. 'How do you know?'

'I saw it.'

'Where?' asked Jo.

'Pocket. What's wrong, don't you like it?'

'Of course not. It's stupid! What would Meg say if she knew?'

'You mustn't tell anyone,' said Laurie.

'I didn't promise,' Jo reminded him.

'I thought you would be pleased,' he said.

'Pleased at the idea of someone coming to take Meg away?' said Jo. 'No, thank you.'

She ran off down the hill, but Laurie came after her and reached the bottom first. She came up behind him, her face red and her hair blowing in the wind.

'That was fun!' she said, forgetting her crossness in the enjoyment of a good run.

At that moment, someone passed by, then stopped and looked back. It was Meg.

'What are you doing here?' she said when she saw Jo. 'You've been running, haven't you? Jo, when *will* you start to behave like a young lady?'

'Don't make me grow up yet, Meg,' said Jo, looking sad. 'It's hard enough having you change so suddenly.'

Meg was growing into a woman, and Laurie's secret

made Jo realize that Meg would leave home one day, perhaps soon.

Two Saturdays after Jo had gone secretly into town, Meg saw Laurie chasing Jo all over the garden before the two of them fell on the grass, laughing and waving a newspaper.

Meg saw Laurie chasing Jo all over the garden.

'What can we do with that girl?' said Meg. 'She never *will* behave like a young lady.'

Minutes later, Jo came in with the newspaper. She sat down and began to read it.

'Are you reading anything interesting?' asked Meg.

'Only a story,' said Jo.

'Read it aloud,' said Amy. 'It may amuse us.'

Jo began to read very fast, and the girls listened. It was a love story about two people called Viola and Angelo, and most of the characters died in the end. But the girls enjoyed it, and Meg even cried a little at the sad parts.

'Who wrote it?' asked Beth, watching Jo's face.

Jo put down the newspaper. 'I did,' she said, her eyes bright and shining.

'You?' said Meg, surprised.

'It's very good,' said Amy.

'I knew it!' said Beth. She ran across and put her arms around her sister. 'Oh, Jo, I *am* so proud!'

And how proud Mrs March was when she was told.

Everyone began to speak at the same time. 'Tell us all about it.' 'How much did you get for it?' 'What will Father say?' 'Won't Laurie laugh!'

So Jo told them all about it, and that evening there was no happier or prouder family than the Marches.

10
A telegram

Mrs March, the girls and Laurie were sitting together on a dull November afternoon when Hannah hurried into the room with a telegram. Mrs March read it, then dropped it to the floor, her face white and her hands shaking. Jo picked up the telegram and read it to the others in a frightened voice. *Mrs March: Your husband is very ill. Come at once. S. Hale, Blank Hospital, Washington.*

The girls moved close to their mother. All their happiness had disappeared in a moment.

'I shall go at once,' said Mrs March, 'but it may be too late. Oh, my children!'

For several minutes, there was only the sound of crying, then Hannah hurried away to get things ready for the long journey.

'Where's Laurie?' Mrs March asked.

'Here,' said the boy. 'Oh, let me do something!'

'Send a telegram and say that I'll come at once,' said Mrs March. 'The next train goes early in the morning. Now, I must write a note to Aunt March. Jo, give me that pen and paper.'

Jo knew that the money for the journey must be borrowed from Aunt March, and she too wanted to do something – anything – to help her father.

Laurie went off to take the note to Aunt March and to

send the telegram. Jo went to fetch some things from the shops, and Amy and Meg helped their mother to get ready.

'Father will need good food and wine to help him get better, and there won't be much at the hospital,' said Mrs March. 'Beth, go and ask Mr Laurence for a couple of bottles of wine. I'm not too proud to beg for Father.'

Mr Laurence came back with Beth. He offered to go with Mrs March, but she wouldn't let the old gentleman make the long, tiring journey, although he could see that she would like to have somebody with her. He went away again, saying, 'I'll be back.'

Soon after, Meg saw Mr Brooke by the door.

'I'm very sorry to hear your news, Miss March,' he said gently. 'Mr Laurence and I think it will be a good idea if I travel with your mother.'

'How kind you all are!' said Meg. 'It will be so good to know that there is someone to take care of Mother. Thank you very much!' She put out her hand and smiled gratefully up into his warm brown eyes.

Laurie came back with a letter and money from Aunt March, but Jo did not return. It was late afternoon when she came walking in and gave her mother some money.

'That's to help make Father comfortable and to bring him home,' she said.

'Twenty-five dollars!' said Mrs March. 'My dear, where did you get it?'

Jo took off her hat.

'Your hair, your beautiful hair!' cried Amy.

All Jo's lovely, thick, long hair was cut short.

'Jo, how could you?' cried Meg.

'My dear girl, there was no need for this,' said Mrs March.

'She doesn't look like my Jo, but I love her dearly for doing it!' said Beth, and began to cry.

Jo wanted to do something for her father.

'Don't cry, Beth,' said Jo. 'I wanted to do something for Father, and selling my hair was the only thing I could think of doing. I'll soon have a curly head again, which will be short and easy to keep tidy.'

But later, when Amy and Beth were asleep and Meg was lying awake, she heard Jo crying.

'Are you crying about Father, Jo?' she asked.

'No, not now. It's my hair,' cried Jo. 'I'd do it again, if I could. But I did love my hair, and the selfish bit of me is making me cry. Don't tell anyone. I'll be all right in the morning.'

During the days after their mother and Mr Brooke went away, Meg and Jo went back to their jobs, and Beth and Amy helped Hannah to keep the house tidy. Everyone tried very hard to be good and hard-working and helpful.

News of their father came through, at first telling them he was dangerously ill, but then saying he was slowly getting better.

Beth

Ten days after their mother went away, Beth came home late after one of several visits to a sick baby at the Hummels' house. She went straight to her mother's room and shut herself inside. Half an hour later, Jo found her sitting there, looking very ill.

'Beth, what's the matter?' cried Jo.

Beth put out a hand to keep her away. 'You've had scarlet fever, haven't you?' she said.

'Years ago, when Meg did,' said Jo. 'Why?'

'Oh, Jo! Mrs Hummel's baby is dead,' said Beth. 'It died in my arms before Mrs Hummel got home.'

'My poor Beth, how awful for you!' said Jo, putting an arm around her sister. 'What did you do?'

'I just sat and held it until Mrs Hummel came with the doctor. He looked at Heinrich and Minna who were also feeling sick. "It's scarlet fever," he said. Then he told me to come home and take some medicine quickly or I would catch it, too.'

'I'll fetch Hannah,' said Jo.

'Don't let Amy come,' said Beth. 'She hasn't had it, and I don't want to give it to her.'

It was decided that Amy must go to Aunt March's house, so Laurie took her there. Poor Amy did not like this plan at all and only agreed to go when Laurie said he would visit her every day to bring her news of Beth.

When Laurie got back, he asked Jo and Meg if he ought to send a telegram to Mrs March.

'Hannah says Mother can't leave Father and would only worry,' said Meg. 'She says Beth won't be sick long, and that she knows what to do, but it doesn't seem right.'

Mr Laurence was not allowed to see Beth, and Meg felt unhappy writing letters to her mother saying nothing about Beth's illness. Jo nursed Beth night and day, but the time came when Beth did not know her and called for her mother. Jo was frightened, and Meg begged to be allowed to write the truth, but Hannah said there was no danger *yet*. Then a letter came saying that Mr March was worse and could not think of coming home for a long time.

How dark the days seemed. How sad and lonely. The sisters worked and waited as the shadow of death lay over the once happy home. It was then that Meg realized how rich she had been in the things which really mattered – love, peace, good health. And Jo, watching her little sister, thought about how unselfish Beth always was – living for others and trying to make home a happy place for all who came there. Amy, sad and lonely at Aunt March's house, just wanted to come home so that she could do something to help Beth.

On the first day of December, the doctor came in the morning. He looked at Beth, then said quietly, 'If Mrs March can leave her husband, I think she should come home now.'

Jo threw on her coat and ran out into the snow to send a telegram. When she arrived back, Laurie came with a letter saying that Mr March was getting better again. This was good news, but Jo's face was so unhappy that Laurie asked, 'What is it? Is Beth worse?'

'I've sent for Mother,' said Jo, beginning to cry. 'Beth doesn't know us any more.'

Laurie held her hand and whispered, 'I'm here, Jo. Hold on to me. Your mother will be here soon, and then everything will be all right.'

'I'm glad Father is better,' said Jo. 'Now Mother won't feel so bad about coming home.'

'You're very tired,' said Laurie. 'But I'll tell you something to cheer you up better than anything.'

'What is it?' said Jo.

Laurie smiled. 'I sent a telegram to your mother *yesterday*, and Mr Brooke answered that she'd come at once. She'll be here tonight and everything will be all right!'

Jo threw her arms around him. 'Oh, Laurie! Oh, Mother! I *am* so glad!' She did not cry again, but held on to her friend. He was surprised, but he smoothed her hair and followed this with a kiss or two.

Jo pushed him gently away. 'Oh, don't! I didn't mean–!'

'I enjoyed it!' laughed Laurie, then went on, 'Grandfather and I thought your mother ought to know. She wouldn't forgive us if Beth – well, if anything happened. Her train will be in at two o'clock in the morning, and I'll meet her.'

All that day, the snow fell and the hours went slowly by. The doctor came, then said he would come back after midnight when he expected there to be some change in Beth's condition, for better or worse. Hannah fell asleep in a chair beside Beth's bed. Mr Laurence waited downstairs, while Laurie lay on the floor pretending to rest. The girls just waited, unable to sleep.

At twelve o'clock, a change seemed to pass over Beth's face. Hannah slept on, but the girls saw the shadow which seemed to fall upon the little bed. An hour went by and Laurie left quietly for the station.

At two o'clock, Jo was standing at the window, watching the snow. She heard something and turned to see Meg kneeling beside her mother's chair. A cold feeling of fear passed over Jo. 'Beth is dead,' she thought.

She ran to the bed. The pain had gone from Beth's face, and now there was a look of peace instead. Jo kissed her and softly whispered, 'Goodbye, Beth, goodbye!'

Hannah woke up and looked at Beth. 'The fever's gone!' she cried. 'She's sleeping and breathing easily!'

The doctor came soon after. 'I think she'll be all right,' he said. 'Keep the house quiet and let her sleep.'

Meg and Jo held each other close, their hearts too full for words. Beth was lying as she used to, with her cheek on her hand, and breathing quietly.

'I wish Mother would come now,' whispered Jo.

And a moment later, they heard the sound of the door below, a cry from Hannah, then Laurie's happy voice saying, 'Girls, she's come! She's come!'

12

Love and Mr Brooke

When Beth woke from her long sleep, she looked into her mother's face and smiled. Then she slept again, but Mrs March held on to her daughter's thin little hand.

Hannah made breakfast while Meg and Jo listened as their mother told them about their father's health, and Mr Brooke's promise to stay with him. Then Meg and Jo closed their tired eyes and were able to rest at last.

Meg and Jo held each other close.

Laurie went to give the good news to Amy at Aunt March's house. He, too, was tired after the long night, and just managed to finish telling his story before he fell asleep in the chair.

Amy began to write a short letter to her mother, but before she could finish it, she saw Mrs March coming towards her aunt's house! Amy ran to meet her.

There were probably many happy little girls in the city that day, but Amy was the happiest of them all as she sat on her mother's knee. 'I've been thinking a lot about Beth,' she said. 'Everyone loves her because she isn't selfish. People wouldn't feel half so bad about me if I was sick, but I'd like to be loved and missed. I'm going to try and be like Beth as much as I can.'

Her mother kissed her. 'I'm sure you will succeed,' she said. 'Now I must go back to Beth. Be patient, little daughter, and we'll soon have you home again.'

That evening, while Meg was writing to her father, Jo went upstairs to Beth's room and found her mother beside the bed, as the little girl slept.

'I want to tell you something, Mother,' said Jo.

'Is it about Meg?' said Mrs March.

'How quickly you guessed!' said Jo. 'Yes, it's about her. Last summer, Meg lost one of her gloves at the Laurences' picnic, and later Laurie told me that Mr Brooke had it, and kept it in his coat pocket. It fell out once, and Laurie saw it. Mr Brooke told Laurie that he liked Meg but was afraid to tell her because she was so young and he was so poor. Isn't it all *awful*?'

'Do you think Meg likes and cares about him?' asked Mrs March, with a worried look.

'I don't know anything about love!' said Jo.

'Do you think she's *not* interested in John?' said Mrs March.

'Who?' said Jo, staring.

'Mr Brooke,' said her mother. 'I call him John because we became good friends at the hospital.'

'Oh, dear!' said Jo. 'He's been good to Father, and now you'll let Meg marry him, if she wants to.'

'My dear, don't be angry,' said Mrs March. 'John told us quite honestly that he loved Meg, but said he would earn enough money for a comfortable home before he asked her to marry him. He wants very much to make her love him if he can. He's an excellent young man, but your father and I will not agree to Meg marrying before she is twenty.'

'I want her to marry Laurie, and be rich,' said Jo.

'I'm afraid Laurie isn't grown-up enough for Meg,' said Mrs March. 'Don't make plans, Jo. Let time and their own hearts bring your friends together.'

Meg came in with the letter for her father.

'Beautifully written, my dear,' said her mother, looking at the letter. 'Please add that I send my love to John.'

'Do you call him John?' said Meg, smiling.

'Yes, he's been like a son to us and we are very fond of him,' said Mrs March, watching her daughter closely.

'I'm glad of that, because he's so lonely,' was Meg's quiet answer. 'Goodnight, Mother dear.'

Mrs March kissed her gently. 'She does not love John yet,' she thought, 'but she will soon learn to.'

13
Laurie makes trouble
and Jo makes peace

Laurie quickly realized that Jo was keeping a secret which she refused to tell him, but he guessed the secret was about Meg and Mr Brooke, and was annoyed that his tutor had said nothing. He began to make some private plans of his own.

Meg, meanwhile, was busy getting things ready for her father's return, but a change suddenly seemed to come over her. For a day or two, she jumped when she was spoken to, and there was a worried look on her face.

Then a letter arrived for her, and a few minutes later Mrs March and Jo saw Meg staring at it with a frightened face.

'My child, what is it?' said Mrs March.

'It's a mistake – he didn't send it. Jo, how could you do it?' Meg hid her face in her hands and cried.

'Me? I've done nothing,' said Jo. 'What's she talking about?'

Meg pulled another letter from her pocket and threw it at Jo. 'You wrote it, and that bad boy helped you. How could you be so cruel and mean to us both?'

Jo and her mother read the letter which had been in Meg's pocket.

My dearest Meg, I can no longer hide my love for you, and must know your answer before I return. I cannot tell

59

your parents yet, but I think they will agree if they know that we love one another. Mr Laurence will help me find a good job, and then, my sweet girl, you will make me happy. Say nothing to your family yet, but send a word of hope to me through Laurie. Your loving John.

'That terrible boy!' said Jo. 'I'll make him sorry.'

But her mother said, 'Wait, Jo. Are you sure this is nothing to do with you?'

'I never saw the letter before!' said Jo. 'But Mr Brooke wouldn't write stupid things like that.'

'It's like his writing,' said Meg unhappily, looking at the second letter in her hand.

'Oh, Meg, you didn't answer it?' said Mrs March.

'Yes, I did!' cried Meg, hiding her face again.

'Let me get that wicked boy!' shouted Jo.

Mrs March sat beside Meg. 'Tell me everything.'

'Laurie brought the first letter,' said Meg. 'He didn't seem to know anything about it. I was going to tell you, but I remembered how you liked Mr Brooke and thought it would be all right to keep my little secret for a while. Now I can never look him in the face again.'

'What did you write to him?' asked Mrs March.

'I only said that I was too young to do anything, and that I didn't wish to have secrets from you so he must speak to Father. I thanked him for his kindness and said I would be his friend, but nothing more, for a long time.'

Mrs March smiled and looked pleased.

Jo laughed. 'What did he reply to that?'

'He writes here that he never sent any love letter, and is sorry that my sister Jo should play games with us like this,' said Meg. 'It's a very kind letter, but imagine how awful I feel.'

'I don't believe Brooke saw either of those letters,' said Jo. 'Laurie wrote them both and he's keeping yours because I won't tell him my secret.'

'Go and fetch Laurie, Jo,' said Mrs March. 'I'll put a stop to all this at once.'

Away ran Jo, and Mrs March gently told Meg Mr Brooke's real feelings. 'Now, dear, do you love him enough to wait until he can make a home for you?'

'I'm frightened and worried,' answered Meg. 'I don't want anything to do with love for a long time – perhaps never. If John *doesn't* know about all this, don't tell him, and please make Jo and Laurie keep quiet.'

Mrs March tried to calm her daughter, but as soon as Meg heard Laurie coming back with Jo, she ran out of the room, and Mrs March saw the boy alone. When Laurie saw Mrs March's angry face, he guessed the reason. Jo waited outside the room as, inside, the voices rose and fell for half an hour. But the girls never knew what was said.

When they were called in, Laurie apologized to Meg, and told her that Mr Brooke knew nothing about either of the two letters. 'Please forgive me, Meg,' he said.

'I'll try,' said Meg, 'but I didn't think you could be so unkind.'

Laurie looked so sorry that Jo wanted to forgive him

straight away, but she said nothing and refused even to look at him. When he went away, looking hurt and unhappy, Jo wished she had been more forgiving. She could never stay angry for long, so after a while she hurried over to the big house, taking with her as an excuse one of Mr Laurence's books that she had borrowed.

'Is Mr Laurence in?' Jo asked a servant.

'Yes, miss, but you can't see him,' said the servant.

'Why? Is he ill?' said Jo.

'No, miss, but he's been arguing with Mr Laurie.'

'Where's Laurie?' said Jo.

'He's shut in his room, and he won't come out.'

'I'll go and see what's the matter,' said Jo. 'I'm not afraid of either of them.'

She went upstairs and knocked on Laurie's door.

'Stop that!' shouted Laurie.

Jo immediately knocked again and the door flew open. She stepped inside before Laurie could stop her. 'I've come to say that I forgive you,' she said, 'and I won't stay angry with you.'

'Oh,' said Laurie. 'Thank you.'

'What's wrong?' she said, seeing his unhappy face.

'I wouldn't tell Grandfather why your mother wanted to see me, because I promised her not to tell anyone,' he said. 'But then Grandfather tried to shake the truth out of me, so I came up here and shut myself in.'

'I expect he's sorry he did that,' said Jo. 'Go down and say *you're* sorry. I'll help you.'

'Grandfather tried to shake the truth out of me.'

'No, I won't!' said Laurie angrily. 'I *was* sorry about Meg, and I asked her to forgive me, but I won't do it again when I'm not the one who is wrong. He ought to believe me when I say I can't tell him something. I don't like being shaken like that, and I won't go down until he apologizes.'

'Listen, if I get your grandfather to apologize for shaking you, will you go down?' said Jo.

'Yes, but you won't do it,' answered Laurie.

'If I can manage the young one, then I can manage the old one,' Jo said to herself as she went downstairs.

'Come in!' said Mr Laurence, when she knocked on his door.

'It's me, sir,' said Jo. 'I'm returning a book.'

'Do you want any more?' said the old man, looking annoyed but trying not to show it.

'Yes, please,' said Jo. And she pretended to look for another book while Mr Laurence stared at her crossly.

'What's that boy been doing?' he asked suddenly. 'He won't tell me.'

'He did do something wrong and we forgave him,' said Jo, 'but we all promised not to say a word to anyone.'

'He must not hide behind a promise from you soft-hearted girls,' said the old gentleman. 'Tell me, Jo.'

'I can't, sir, because Mother has ordered me not to,' said Jo. 'And if I tell you, it will make trouble for someone else, not Laurie.'

This seemed to calm the old man. 'Then I'll forgive him,' he said after a moment. 'He's a difficult boy and hard to manage, you know.'

'So am I,' said Jo, 'but a kind word always helps.'

'You think I'm not kind to him?' he said sharply.

'Too kind, very often,' said Jo, a little afraid, 'but just a bit quick to be angry with him sometimes.'

The old gentleman looked a little ashamed. 'You're right, I am. Although I love the boy, I find it hard to be patient with him sometimes. Bring him down and tell him it's all right. I'm sorry I shook him.'

'Why not write him an apology, sir?' said Jo. 'He says he won't come down until he's got one.'

Mr Laurence gave her another sharp look, but then smiled and put on his glasses. 'Here, give me a bit of paper,' he said.

The words were written and Jo kissed the old man's

cheek. Then she went upstairs and put the letter under Laurie's door. But he came out before she was gone.

'Well done, Jo,' he said. 'Did he shout at you?'

'No, he was quite calm,' said Jo. 'Now, go and eat your dinner. You'll both feel better after it.'

Everyone thought the matter was ended, but although others forgot it, Meg remembered. She never talked about Laurie's tutor but she thought of him often and dreamed her dreams. And once, when Jo was looking for something in her sister's desk, she found a bit of paper with 'Mrs John Brooke' written on it over and over again.

'Oh, dear!' said Jo.

⚬⚬14⚬⚬
Happier days

Christmas Day was very different that year. Beth felt much better and was carried to the window to see the snowman which Jo and Laurie had made. It had a basket of fruit and flowers in one hand and a new piece of music in the other. Laurie ran up and down, bringing in the presents, and Jo sang a funny song.

'I'm so happy!' laughed Beth, as Jo carried her back to the other room to rest after the fun. 'Oh, I do wish that Father was here too!'

Half an hour later, Laurie came to the house and opened the door quietly. 'Here's another Christmas present for the March family!' he called out.

He moved away, and in his place appeared a tall man holding the arm of another tall man, who tried to say something but couldn't.

'Father!' cried Meg and Jo together – and Mr March disappeared under lots of loving arms and kisses. Mr Brooke kissed Meg – by mistake, as he tried to explain.

Suddenly, the door to the other room opened, and there was Beth, running straight into her father's arms. There were tears of happiness on many faces before all the excitement died down. Then Mrs March thanked Mr Brooke for taking care of her husband, and he and Laurie left the family to themselves.

'Here's another Christmas present for the March family!'

Mr March and Beth sat in one big armchair, and the others sat around them. 'I wanted to surprise you all, and the doctor let Mr Brooke bring me home,' said Mr March. 'John has been so good to me. He is an excellent young man.' Mr March looked at Meg, who was staring at the fire, then he smiled at his wife. She smiled back. Jo understood exactly what the smiles were saying, and went out to the kitchen complaining to herself about 'excellent young men with brown eyes!'

There never *was* a Christmas dinner like the one they had that day. Mr Laurence and his grandson ate with them, and so did Mr Brooke. Jo gave the tutor many black looks and would not speak to him, which amused Laurie.

The guests left early and the happy family sat together around the fire.

'A year ago we were complaining about the awful Christmas we expected to have, do you remember?' said Jo.

'It's been quite a good year,' said Meg, thinking about Mr Brooke.

'I think it's been a hard one,' said Amy.

'I'm glad it's over, because we've got Father back,' whispered Beth, who was sitting on his knee.

'I've discovered several things about you young ladies today,' said Mr March.

'Oh, tell us what they are!' cried Meg.

'Here's one,' he said, taking her hand. It had a small burn on the back and two or three little hard places on the front.

'I remember when this hand was white and smooth. It was pretty then, but to me it's much prettier now. I'm proud of this hard-working hand, Meg.'

'What about Jo?' whispered Beth. 'She's tried so hard, and has been very, very good to me.'

He smiled and looked at Jo sitting opposite. 'Her hair may be short, but I see a young lady now. Her face is thin and white from worrying, but it has grown gentler. Perhaps I'll miss my wild girl, but I'm sure I'll love the warm-hearted woman who has taken her place.'

Jo's face was red in the firelight as she listened.

'Now Beth,' said Amy.

'She's not as shy as she used to be,' said her father lovingly, and he held Beth close when he remembered how near they had come to losing her. Then he looked down at Amy by his feet. 'I've noticed today that Amy has helped everyone patiently and with a smile. She's learned to think more about other people, and less about herself.'

Beth moved out of her father's arms and went to the piano. She touched the keys softly and began to sing. Soon, the others joined her in a happy Christmas song.

The next afternoon, Jo and Meg were sitting at the window when Laurie went by. When he saw Meg, he fell on one knee in the snow, beat his chest, and put out his arms towards her. When Meg told him to go away, he pretended to cry before walking away looking miserable.

Meg laughed. 'What was he doing?' she said.

'He was showing you how your John will act,' answered Jo, crossly.

'Don't say *my John*, it isn't right.' But Meg said the words again silently inside her head.

'If he asks you to marry him, you'll cry or look stupid, instead of saying a loud No,' said Jo.

'No, I won't,' said Meg. 'I'll say, "Thank you, Mr Brooke, you are very kind, but I am too young to marry you. Please let us be friends, as we were."'

'I don't believe it,' said Jo.

'It's true. Then I'll walk out of the room with my head high.' Meg got up and pretended to do it – but ran back to her seat when she heard someone knock on the door.

Jo opened it with an angry look.

'Good afternoon,' said Mr Brooke. 'I came to get my umbrella, which I left behind yesterday.'

'I'll get it,' said Jo, pushing past him. 'Now Meg can tell him,' she thought.

But Meg was moving to the door. 'I expect Mother will want to see you,' she said. 'I'll call her.'

'Don't go,' he said. 'Are you afraid of me, Meg?'

'How can I be afraid when you've been so kind to Father,' said Meg. 'I wish I could thank you for it.'

'You can,' he said. And he took Meg's small hand in his and looked at her lovingly.

'Oh, please don't,' she said, looking frightened.

'I only want to know if you love me a little, Meg,' he said gently. 'I love you so much.'

This was the moment to repeat the words she had told Jo, but Meg forgot them all. 'I don't know,' she said, so softly that John had to move closer to hear her reply.

He smiled gratefully. 'Will you try to find out?'

'I'm too young,' she said, hesitating but feeling her heart beating rather fast.

'I'll wait while you learn to like me,' he said. 'Will it be very difficult?'

'Not if I choose to learn,' she said.

'Please choose, Meg. I love to teach, and this is easier than German,' said John, taking her other hand.

She looked at him and saw that he was smiling. He seemed so sure of success that Meg became a little annoyed. She felt excited and strange, and taking her hands away from his, she said, 'I *don't* choose. Please go away!'

Poor Mr Brooke looked shocked. 'Do you mean that?'

'Yes,' she said, rather enjoying the game she was playing. 'I don't want to think about these things. It's too soon.'

'I'll wait until you've had more time,' he said, and looked so unhappy that Meg began to feel sorry for him.

It was at this moment that Aunt March came in. She had come to see Mr March and was hoping to surprise the family. She *did* surprise two of them. Meg, with her face bright red, just stared at her aunt, while Mr Brooke hurried into another room.

'Goodness me, what's all this?' cried Aunt March.

'It's Father's friend,' said Meg hurriedly. 'I'm *so* surprised to see you, Aunt March.'

At this moment Aunt March came in.

'I can see that,' said Aunt March, sitting down. 'What has he said to make your face turn pink?'

'Mr Brooke and I were just . . . talking,' said Meg.

'Brooke? The boy's tutor? I understand now. I know all about it because I made Jo tell me. You haven't promised to marry him, have you, Meg? If you have, you won't get one bit of my money, do you hear?'

It was exactly the wrong thing to say. When Meg was *ordered* not to marry John Brooke, she immediately decided that she *would*. 'I'll marry whoever I want to, Aunt March, and you can give your money to anyone you like!' she said.

'You'll be sorry!' said Aunt March. 'Why don't you marry a rich man to help your family?'

'Father and Mother like John, although he's poor,' said Meg.

'Be sensible, Meg,' said her aunt. 'He knows I have money, and that's why he likes you, I suspect.'

'Don't say that!' said Meg. 'My John wouldn't marry for money any more than I would! We'll work and wait, and I'll be happy with him because he loves me, and—'

Meg stopped as she remembered that she had told 'her John' to go away.

Aunt March was very angry. 'Just don't expect anything from me when you are married!' she said. And she went out of the room, banging the door behind her.

Meg didn't know whether to laugh or cry. Before she could decide, Mr Brooke came back in from the next room and put his arms around her. 'Oh Meg, I could hear your voices,' he said. 'Thank you for proving that you do love me a little.'

'I didn't know how much until she said those things about you,' said Meg.

'So I can stay, and be happy?' he said.

'Yes, John,' she whispered, and hid her face on John's chest.

Jo returned and found them like that. Meg jumped and turned round, but John Brooke laughed and kissed the shocked Jo, saying, 'Sister Jo. Wish us luck!'

Jo ran upstairs to find her parents. 'Go down quickly!' she said. 'John Brooke is behaving terribly and Meg likes it!'

Mr and Mrs March left the room in a hurry, while Jo threw herself on the bed and told the awful news to Beth and Amy. But the little girls thought it was all most interesting and delightful.

Nobody knew what was said that afternoon, but a lot of talking was done. The quiet Mr Brooke managed to persuade his friends that his plans were good and sensible, then he proudly took Meg in to supper. Everyone looked so happy that Jo tried to look pleased too.

After supper, Laurie arrived with some flowers for 'Mrs John Brooke', then he followed Jo into the corner of the room while the others went to welcome old Mr Laurence.

'What's the matter, Jo?' said Laurie. 'You don't look very happy.'

'Nothing will ever be the same again,' said Jo sadly. 'I've lost my dearest friend.'

'You've got me,' said Laurie. 'I'm not good for much, but I promise I'll always be your friend, Jo.'

'I know you will,' answered Jo, gratefully.

'Then don't be sad,' he said. 'I'll be back from college in three years' time, and then we'll go abroad, or on a nice trip somewhere. Wouldn't that cheer you up?'

'Anything can happen in three years,' said Jo.

'That's true,' said Laurie. 'Don't you wish you knew what was going to happen?'

'I don't think so,' said Jo. 'It may be something sad, and everyone looks so happy now.' As she spoke, she looked round the room, and her face brightened at the sight.

Father and Mother sat happily together. Amy was drawing a picture of Meg and John, who were looking lovingly at each other. Beth lay on the floor, talking to her old friend, Mr Laurence. Jo sat in her favourite chair with a serious, quiet look on her face. Laurie smiled at her in the long mirror that was opposite them both. And Jo smiled back.

GLOSSARY

complain to say crossly that you do not like something

forgive to say or show that you are not angry with someone any more

gossip *(v and n)* to talk about other people, often unkindly

grow up to become an adult

look after to take care of someone or something

perfume a sweet-smelling liquid, which you put on your body

picnic a meal eaten outside, away from home

play *(n)* a story that is acted in a theatre, on television or radio, etc.

print *(v)* to put words on paper (books, newspapers, etc.) using a machine

servant someone who is paid to work in another person's house

shocked surprised, by something terrible or not at all nice

skates boots with a piece of metal fixed underneath for moving on ice

telegram a message sent very quickly by electricity or radio

toy a plaything for a child

tutor a private teacher for a child or children at their home

war fighting between countries, or between large groups of people in the same country

wicked very bad or wrong

wine an alcoholic drink made from grapes

Little Women

ACTIVITIES

Before Reading

1 **Read the story introduction on the first page of the book, and the back cover. How much do you know now about the story? Complete each sentence with the right name.**

Meg / Jo / Beth / Amy

1 _____ is afraid of talking to people she doesn't know.

2 _____ sometimes gets into fights when she is angry.

3 _____ is unhappy because she hasn't got any nice clothes.

4 _____ is often selfish.

5 _____ will try in future to enjoy her work.

6 _____ would rather be a boy than a girl.

7 _____ is the youngest of the March girls.

8 _____ is a quiet girl who likes being by herself.

2 **What are the 'troubles and difficulties' that are waiting for the girls? Can you guess? Choose some of these ideas.**

1 One of the girls gets a dangerous illness and nearly dies.

2 Two of the girls have a fight and one of them is hurt.

3 Their father dies in the war and never comes home.

4 Their mother has to go away to look after their father.

5 One of the girls burns something belonging to her sister.

6 Two of the girls fall in love with the boy next door.

7 One of the girls makes some very unsuitable friends.

8 One of the girls wants to stop her sister getting married.

While Reading

Read Chapters 1 to 3. Choose the best question-word for these questions, and then answer them.

How / What / Where

1 . . . was the girls' father?
2 . . . had the family become poor?
3 . . . did the girls decide to do about Christmas presents?
4 . . . did the girls help the Hummel family?
5 . . . happened in the middle of the Christmas play?
6 . . . did old Mr Laurence do for the girls, and why?
7 . . . disasters happened to Jo and Meg on New Year's Eve?
8 . . . did the party end for Jo and Meg?

Read Chapters 4 to 6. Here are some untrue sentences about these chapters. Change them into true sentences.

1 Meg and Jo had jobs because they wanted money to spend.
2 Jo visited Laurie because he was ill and needed nursing.
3 Mr Laurence was annoyed by Laurie's friendship with the Marches, and thought he should work hard at his studies.
4 Mr Laurence gave Beth a piano because he liked her playing so much.
5 Amy was so angry with Jo that she threw Jo's skates away.
6 When Amy begged for forgiveness, Jo forgave her.
7 Jo warned Amy about the thin ice, but Amy didn't listen.

Read Chapters 7 and 8. Who said this, and to whom? Who, or what, were they talking about?

1 'We didn't know you had a young man.'
2 'It would be an excellent thing for one of those girls.'
3 'I didn't know you, because you look so unlike yourself.'
4 'I'm a doll who does crazy things.'
5 'She says we must look after ourselves today.'
6 'Isn't it better to have time for play *and* time for work?'
7 'We would all be very sorry if anything happened to you.'

Before you read Chapter 9, can you guess what happens? Circle the names and words that you think are correct.

Mr Brooke / Laurie falls in love with *Jo / Meg*. Soon after, *Amy / Jo / Laurie* finds out and tells the secret to *Mrs March / Beth / Jo*, who is not very *happy / surprised / worried* about it.

Read Chapters 9 to 12, and then answer these questions.

1 What were Jo's and Laurie's secrets?
2 How did the family feel when Jo's story was printed?
3 How did everyone help Mrs March when she heard the news about her husband?
4 How did Beth become ill?
5 Why did Amy have to stay at Aunt March's house?
6 Why didn't Meg tell her mother the truth about Beth?
7 What did Beth's illness teach Meg, Jo, and Amy?
8 How did Mrs March feel about Meg marrying John?

Before you read Chapter 13 (*Laurie makes trouble and Jo makes peace*), can you guess what happens? Choose some of these ideas.

Laurie writes love letters . . .
1 to Mr Brooke, pretending they are from Meg.
2 to Meg, pretending they are from Mr Brooke.
3 to Meg, from himself.
Jo finds out about these letters and . . .
4 is very angry about them.
5 thinks they are very funny.
6 tells everyone about them and gets Laurie into trouble.

Read Chapters 13 and 14. Now fill in the correct names.

1 _____ thought that _____ had written the two letters, but in fact _____ wrote them.

2 _____ made _____ promise not to tell anyone what he had done, but then _____ tried to shake the truth out of _____.

3 _____ and _____ had a big argument about this, but _____ came and made peace between them, by persuading _____ to apologize to _____.

4 _____ brought _____ home on Christmas Day.

5 _____, _____, and _____ joined the March family for Christmas dinner.

6 When _____ told _____ not to marry _____, _____ realized that she did in fact love him.

7 _____ and _____ were delighted about their sister and _____, but _____ felt sad and _____ tried to cheer her up.

After Reading

1 **What do you think Mrs March said to Laurie about the 'love letters' (page 61)? Complete Laurie's side of the conversation.**

MRS MARCH: Now, Laurie, did you write these letters?
LAURIE: _____
MRS MARCH: Well, it's a game that's hurt Meg, and made Jo angry. Who else knows about these letters? Mr Brooke?
LAURIE: _____
MRS MARCH: That's one good thing, I suppose. But I'm very disappointed in you, Laurie. You've been very unkind.
LAURIE: _____
MRS MARCH: I accept that you didn't mean to. But it's not really *me* you should apologize to, is it, Laurie?
LAURIE: _____
MRS MARCH: Good. I'll call her in presently, but first, will you promise me never to talk about this to anyone?
LAURIE: _____

2 **When Mrs March came home, Meg wrote to her father (see page 57). Complete her letter, using as many words as you like.**

Dear Father
We were all very happy to hear that you _____. We have had a very difficult time here, because Beth _____.
I wanted to write to Mother about it, but Hannah said

_____. Amy went _____ and Jo _____.
Yesterday the doctor told us _____, and we all felt
_____. But just before Mother arrived, the fever _____
and Beth _____. Now we are all very tired, of course, but
we are so happy that Beth _____ and that Mother
_____. We all send you our love, and hope _____.

    Your loving Meg

    P.S. Mother has asked me to _____.

3 Can you find the twenty-four words hidden in this word
  search? Words go from left to right, and from top to bottom.

U	N	C	O	M	F	O	R	T	A	B	L	E	F
M	E	A	N	A	L	A	Z	Y	N	G	B	M	S
H	E	L	P	F	U	L	P	S	N	R	R	I	A
A	V	M	W	L	Q	O	S	H	O	A	A	S	D
P	O	L	I	T	E	N	E	O	Y	T	V	E	W
P	P	C	L	Y	S	E	L	C	E	E	E	R	I
Y	R	R	D	N	H	L	F	K	D	F	H	A	C
R	O	U	G	H	Y	Y	I	E	F	U	U	B	K
K	U	E	C	R	O	S	S	D	O	L	R	L	E
R	D	L	W	A	R	M	H	E	A	R	T	E	D

Now put the words into two lists, under these headings. Then
find another five words for each list from the story.

WORDS DESCRIBING WHAT PEOPLE ARE LIKE	WORDS DESCRIBING HOW PEOPLE FEEL

4 **Perhaps some of the characters in the story had these thoughts about the four 'little women' at different times. Which characters are they, which sister were they thinking about, and when?**

1 'What a terrible breakfast! That egg was *black*! Now I hear she's invited Laurie to dinner tonight. I'm sure they'll all enjoy themselves – whatever the food's like – but I think I'll go and have my dinner somewhere else!'

2 'Oh, I do hope she isn't going to be ill too! She's a quiet little thing, but so brave and kind. I'll never forget seeing her sitting there with my poor baby in her arms . . .'

3 'Silly, silly girl! I suppose she thinks she can live on love! Well, she needn't come begging to me when times are hard, because I won't give her a penny. Why don't her parents find somebody rich for her – and quickly?'

4 'There she goes, crossing the hall like a shadow. I've never known a girl so shy! Ah, she's begun playing. I'll just open my study door a bit wider, then I'll hear better . . .'

5 'She's been so lonely, away from her sisters. But she'll soon be able to go home. It was wonderful to see her face just now when I told her the good news. It's been a long night, though. I'll just close my eyes for a second or two . . .'

6 'That girl! I was so angry with the boy, and now she's made *me* write *him* an apology! I don't know. But I'm afraid she's right – I should be more patient . . .'

5 What 'bad' and 'good' things did the girls and Laurie do? Match each prompt to the right character, and write sentences to say what they did, and when or why they did these things.

Meg / Jo / Beth / Amy / Laurie

1 looking after a sick baby
2 love letters
3 party dress and wine
4 warning about thin ice
5 notebook of stories
6 selling her hair
7 big bottle of perfume
8 kind to John Brooke
9 telegram to Mrs March
10 pair of men's slippers

6 What happens next to the characters in *Little Women*? Choose one or more things for each character and write a paragraph about what happens next.

MEG: marries John Brooke / marries Belle's rich brother / becomes rich when Aunt March dies

JO: marries Laurie / marries someone else / becomes a writer

BETH: looks after her parents / dies / becomes a nurse / never marries

AMY: marries a rich businessman / becomes a famous painter / marries Laurie

LAURIE: marries Meg / marries Jo / marries Amy / becomes a musician / goes to Europe

7 Which character did you like best in the book, and which did you like least? Why?

ABOUT THE AUTHOR

Louisa May Alcott was born in 1832 in Pennsylvania, USA, but lived most of her life in Massachusetts. Her father, a well-known philosopher and teacher, encouraged her to write, and by the time of her death in 1888 Louisa had written hundreds of plays, short stories, poems, and novels.

Louisa's father was not good with money, and her strong, loving mother ran the household. Louisa helped to support the family by teaching, nursing, and by writing stories and novels. When a publisher asked her to write a book for girls, Louisa began work on this a little doubtfully, writing in her diary that she 'never liked girls, or knew many, except my sisters'.

Little Women, published in 1868, was a huge success. Louisa used the experiences of her own family – she and her three sisters became the March sisters, Amy, Jo, Beth, and Meg. The story of the March girls continued in *Good Wives*, *Little Men*, and *Jo's Boys*, though not always in ways that readers expected. 'Girls write to ask who the little women marry,' Louisa Alcott wrote, 'as if that was the only end and aim of a woman's life. I *won't* marry Jo to Laurie to please anyone.'

In August 1868 Louisa Alcott received her first copy of *Little Women*. 'It reads better than I expected,' she wrote in her diary. 'Not a bit sensational, but simple and true, for we really lived most of it; and if it succeeds that will be the reason of it.'

Little Women has become a classic of American children's literature. It has never been out of print, and the story has been filmed four times, first as a black and white silent film in 1918, and most recently in 1994, with Winona Ryder as Jo.

ABOUT BOOKWORMS

OXFORD BOOKWORMS LIBRARY
Classics • True Stories • Fantasy & Horror • Human Interest
Crime & Mystery • Thriller & Adventure

The OXFORD BOOKWORMS LIBRARY offers a wide range of original and adapted stories, both classic and modern, which take learners from elementary to advanced level through six carefully graded language stages:

Stage 1 (400 headwords)	**Stage 4** (1400 headwords)
Stage 2 (700 headwords)	**Stage 5** (1800 headwords)
Stage 3 (1000 headwords)	**Stage 6** (2500 headwords)

More than fifty titles are also available on cassette, and there are many titles at Stages 1 to 4 which are specially recommended for younger learners. In addition to the introductions and activities in each Bookworm, resource material includes photocopiable test worksheets and Teacher's Handbooks, which contain advice on running a class library and using cassettes, and the answers for the activities in the books.

Several other series are linked to the OXFORD BOOKWORMS LIBRARY. They range from highly illustrated readers for young learners, to playscripts, non-fiction readers, and unsimplified texts for advanced learners.

Oxford Bookworms Starters   *Oxford Bookworms Factfiles*
Oxford Bookworms Playscripts   *Oxford Bookworms Collection*

Details of these series and a full list of all titles in the OXFORD BOOKWORMS LIBRARY can be found in the *Oxford English* catalogues. A selection of titles from the OXFORD BOOKWORMS LIBRARY can be found on the next pages.

Lorna Doone

R. D. BLACKMORE

Retold by David Penn

One winter's day in 1673 young John Ridd is riding home from school, across the wild lonely hills of Exmoor. He has to pass Doone valley – a dangerous place, as the Doones are famous robbers and murderers. All Exmoor lives in fear of the Doones.

At home there is sad news waiting for young John, and he learns that he has good reason to hate the Doones. But in the years to come he meets Lorna Doone, with her lovely smile and big dark eyes. And soon he is deeply, hopelessly, in love . . .

Black Beauty

ANNA SEWELL

Retold by John Escott

When Black Beauty is trained to carry a rider on his back, or to pull a carriage behind him, he finds it hard at first. But he is lucky – his first home is a good one, where his owners are kind people, who would never be cruel to a horse.

But in the nineteenth century many people *were* cruel to their horses, whipping them and beating them, and using them like machines until they dropped dead. Black Beauty soon finds this out, and as he describes his life, he has many terrible stories to tell.

Cranford

ELIZABETH GASKELL

Retold by Kate Mattock

Life in the small English town of Cranford seems very quiet and peaceful. The ladies of Cranford lead tidy, regular lives. They make their visits between the hours of twelve and three, give little evening parties, and worry about their maid-servants. But life is not always smooth – there are little arguments and jealousies, sudden deaths and unexpected marriages . . .

Mrs Gaskell's timeless picture of small-town life in the first half of the nineteenth century has delighted readers for nearly 150 years.

Washington Square

HENRY JAMES

Retold by Kieran McGovern

When a handsome young man begins to court Catherine Sloper, she feels she is very lucky. She is a quiet, gentle girl, but neither beautiful nor clever; no one had ever admired her before, or come to the front parlour of her home in Washington Square to whisper soft words of love to her.

But in New York in the 1840s young ladies are not free to marry where they please. Catherine must have her father's permission, and Dr Sloper is a rich man. One day Catherine will have a fortune of 30,000 dollars a year . . .

Desert, Mountain, Sea

SUE LEATHER

Three different parts of the world, but all of them dangerous, lonely places. Three different women, but all of them determined to go – and to come back alive!

Robyn Davidson walked nearly 3,000 kilometres across the Australian desert – with a dog and four camels.

Arlene Blum led a team of ten women to the top of Annapurna – one of the highest mountains in the world. Only eight came down again.

Naomi James sailed around the world alone, on a journey lasting more than 250 days.

Three real adventures – three really adventurous women.

The Garden Party and Other Stories

KATHERINE MANSFIELD

Retold by Rosalie Kerr

Oh, how delightful it is to fall in love for the first time! How exciting to go to your first dance when you are a girl of eighteen! But life can also be hard and cruel, if you are young and inexperienced and travelling alone across Europe . . . or if you are a child from the wrong social class . . . or a singer without work and the rent to be paid.

Set in Europe and New Zealand, these nine stories by Katherine Mansfield dig deep beneath the appearances of life to show us the causes of human happiness and despair.